MegaMillions Magic

Secrets To Winning MegaMillions Lotto!

NSW Lotteries

National

Pay FISHER T J

Lotto

$1,008,742.00

From Real-Life DOUBLE Million-Dollar Lotto Winner Terry Fisher.

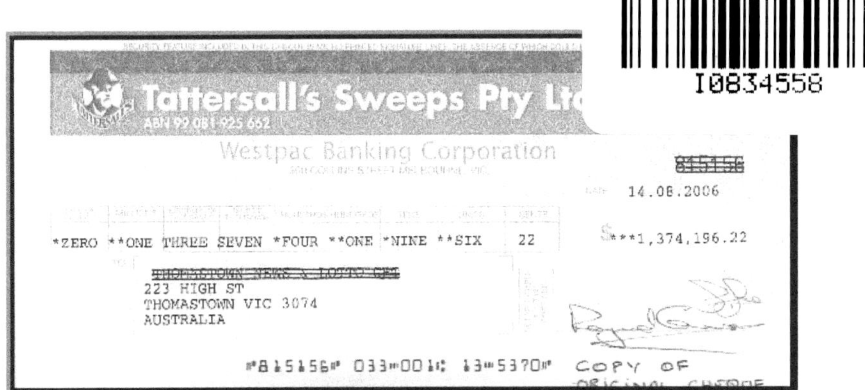

I0834558

Tattersall's Sweeps Pty Ltd

ABN 99 081 925 662

Westpac Banking Corporation

815156

14.08.2006

*ZERO **ONE THREE SEVEN *FOUR **ONE *NINE **SIX 22

$***1,374,196.22

THOMASTOWN NEWS & LOTTO CNT

223 HIGH ST

THOMASTOWN VIC 3074

AUSTRALIA

⑈815156⑈ 033⑆001⑆ 13⑈5370⑈ COPY OF ORIGINAL CHEQUE

Proudly Published by:

Terry Fisher Enterprises,
PO Box 535, Tweed Heads,
NSW 2485, Australia.

Ph: (07) 5534 8322 or 61 755 348 322 (Outside Australia)

Email: *terryf@gldnet.com.au*

OUR OTHER WEBSITES:

http://www.lottery-and-lotto.com

http://www.powerballpro.com

http://www.winninglottoblog.com

http://www.freelottosecrets.com

http://www.winning-the-lottery.com

http://www.lottomasta.com

http://www.lotto-magic.com

http://www.ozlotto7tips.com

http://www.ozlottoblog.com

ISBN No: 978-1-4709-6651-5

We strongly recommend keeping Lotto fun by betting well within your financial limits.

CONTENTS …

We Do Not Want To Brag, But …

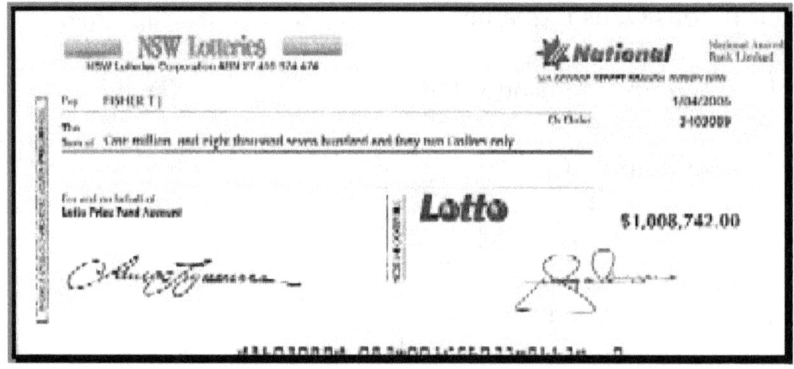

This is our First Million Dollar Win. It was a Syndicate (Lotto Club) Entry that I personally designed and ran.

It played all of the lotto numbers, in multiple System Entries.

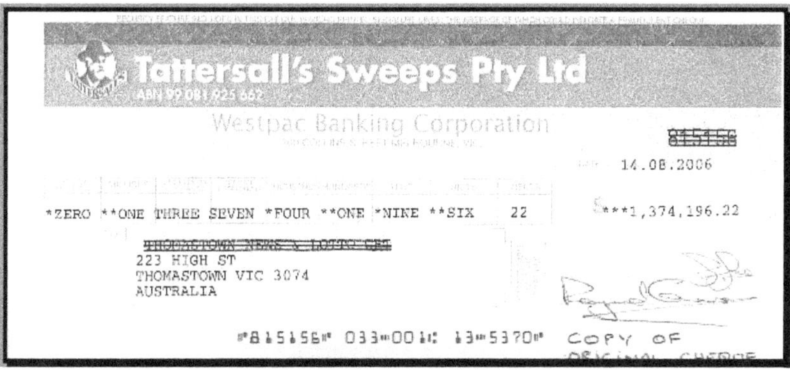

This is our second Lotto First Prize, again a Syndicate (Lotto Club) Entry based on the previous design, playing all the numbers, in multiple System Entries.

By now I had changed from running my Syndicates personally to using a Lotto Agent, Peter Karol.

Just Pure Luck? Maybe – But that probably makes Peter and I the luckiest people on the Planet!

Here are some near misses:

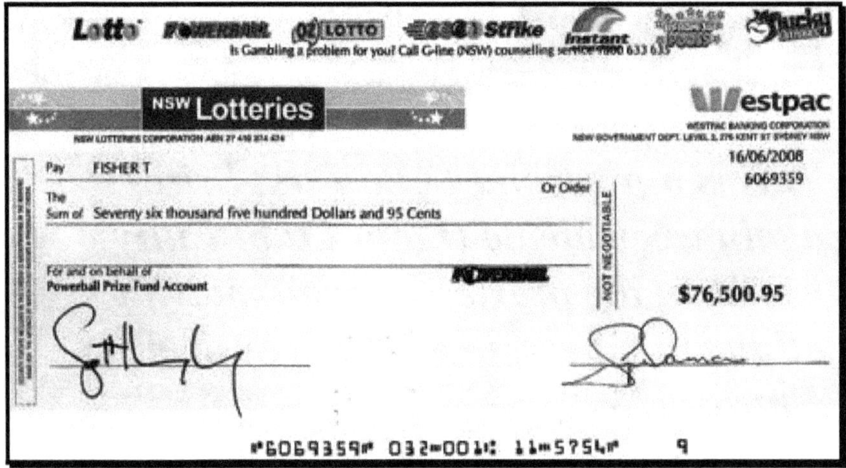

As you can see we won $76,500.95 for 5 numbers in Australian Powerball.

Check the next page – If we had had the Powerball too, we would have shared $58 Million with one other winner !

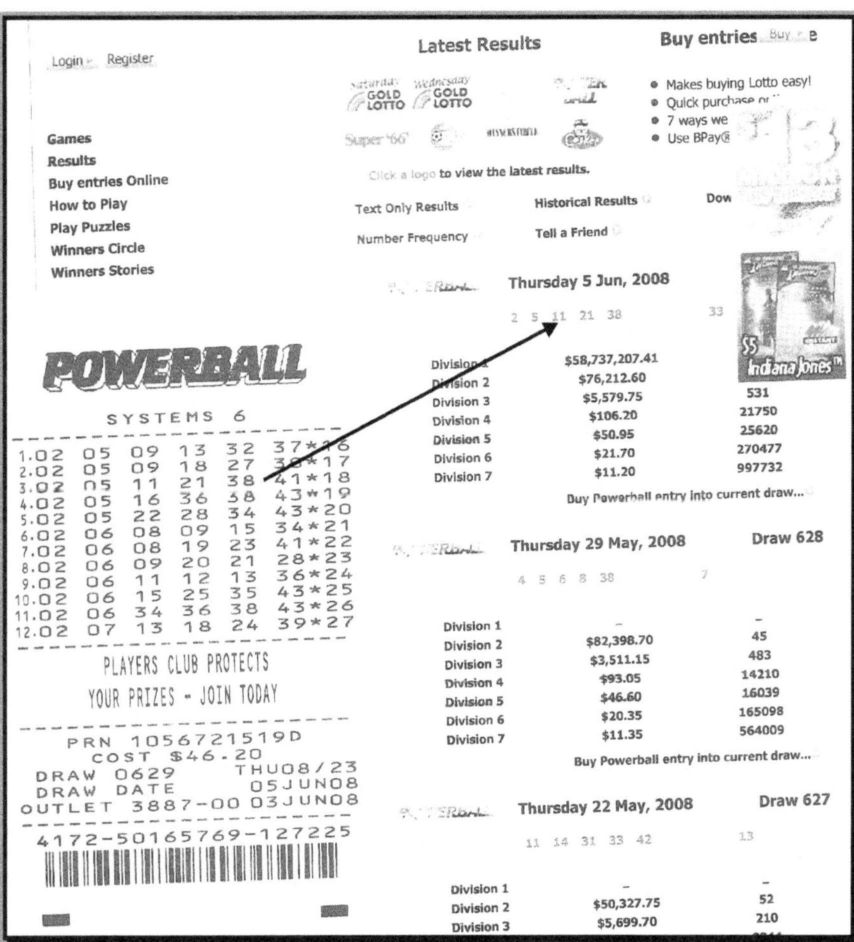
Login Register
Latest Results
Buy entries
Makes buying Lotto easy!
Quick purchase or
7 ways we
Use BPay
GOLD LOTTO
GOLD LOTTO
Games
Results
Buy entries Online
How to Play
Play Puzzles
Winners Circle
Winners Stories
Click a logo to view the latest results.
Text Only Results
Historical Results
Number Frequency
Tell a Friend
Thursday 5 Jun, 2008
2 5 11 21 38 33
Division 1 $58,737,207.41
Division 2 $76,212.60
Division 3 $5,579.75 531
Division 4 $106.20 21750
Division 5 $50.95 25620
Division 6 $21.70 270477
Division 7 $11.20 997732
Buy Powerball entry into current draw...
Indiana Jones
POWERBALL
SYSTEMS 6
1.02 05 09 13 32 37*16
2.02 05 09 18 27 38*17
3.02 05 11 21 38 41*18
4.02 05 16 36 38 43*19
5.02 05 22 28 34 43*20
6.02 06 08 09 15 34*21
7.02 06 08 19 23 41*22
8.02 06 09 20 21 28*23
9.02 06 11 12 13 36*24
10.02 06 15 25 35 43*25
11.02 06 34 36 38 43*26
12.02 07 13 18 24 39*27
PLAYERS CLUB PROTECTS
YOUR PRIZES - JOIN TODAY
PRN 1056721519D
COST $46.20
DRAW 0629 THU08/23
DRAW DATE 05JUN08
OUTLET 3887-00 03JUN08
4172-50165769-127225
Thursday 29 May, 2008 Draw 628
4 5 6 8 38 7
Division 1 - -
Division 2 $82,398.70 45
Division 3 $3,511.15 483
Division 4 $93.05 14210
Division 5 $46.60 16039
Division 6 $20.35 165098
Division 7 $11.35 564009
Buy Powerball entry into current draw...
Thursday 22 May, 2008 Draw 627
11 14 31 33 42 13
Division 1 - -
Division 2 $50,327.75 52
Division 3 $5,699.70 210

But to many people, even wins like this would be welcome:

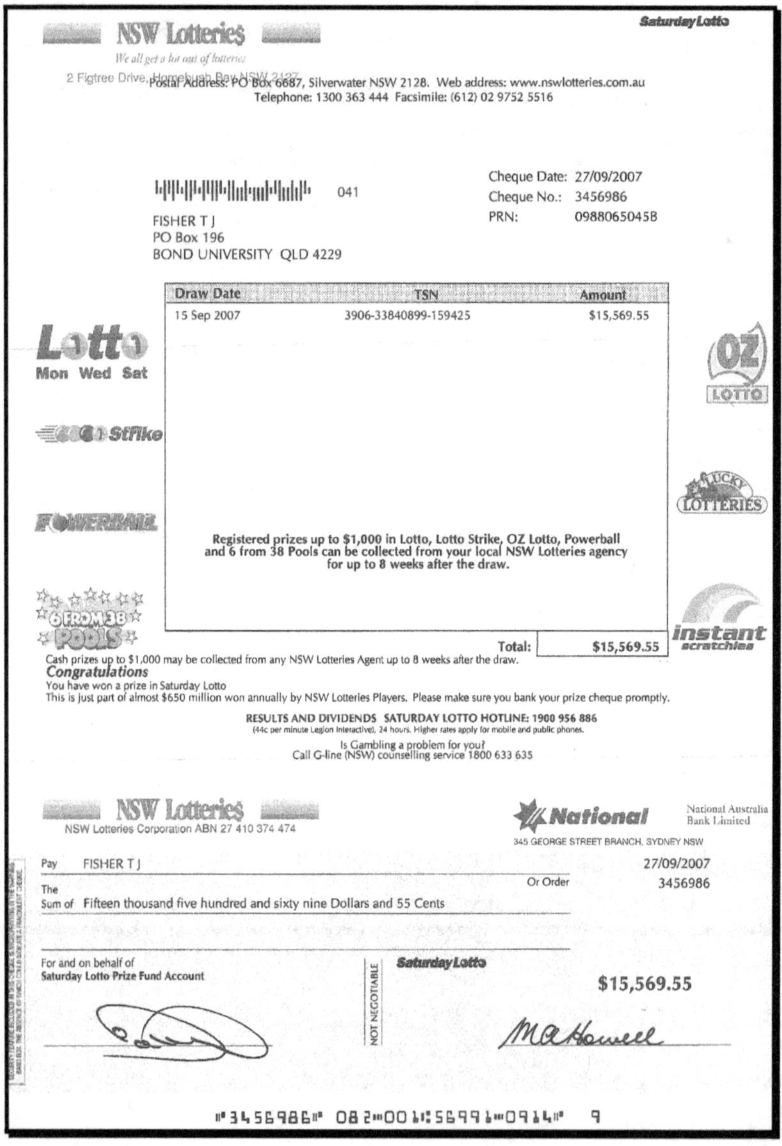

NSW Lotteries

We all get a lot out of lotteries

Saturday Lotto

2 Figtree Drive, Homebush Bay NSW 2127 Postal Address: PO Box 6687, Silverwater NSW 2128. Web address: www.nswlotteries.com.au
Telephone: 1300 363 444 Facsimile: (612) 02 9752 5516

041

FISHER T J
PO Box 196
BOND UNIVERSITY QLD 4229

Cheque Date: 27/09/2007
Cheque No.: 3456986
PRN: 0988065045B

Draw Date	TSN	Amount
15 Sep 2007	3906-33840899-159425	$15,569.55

Registered prizes up to $1,000 in Lotto, Lotto Strike, OZ Lotto, Powerball and 6 from 38 Pools can be collected from your local NSW Lotteries agency for up to 8 weeks after the draw.

Total: $15,569.55

Cash prizes up to $1,000 may be collected from any NSW Lotteries Agent up to 8 weeks after the draw.

Congratulations

You have won a prize in Saturday Lotto

This is just part of almost $650 million won annually by NSW Lotteries Players. Please make sure you bank your prize cheque promptly.

RESULTS AND DIVIDENDS SATURDAY LOTTO HOTLINE: 1900 956 886

(44c per minute Legion Interactive), 24 hours. Higher rates apply for mobile and public phones.

Is Gambling a problem for you?
Call G-line (NSW) counselling service 1800 633 635

NSW Lotteries
NSW Lotteries Corporation ABN 27 410 374 474

National
National Australia Bank Limited
345 GEORGE STREET BRANCH, SYDNEY NSW

Pay FISHER T J

27/09/2007
Or Order 3456986

The Sum of Fifteen thousand five hundred and sixty nine Dollars and 55 Cents

For and on behalf of
Saturday Lotto Prize Fund Account

NOT NEGOTIABLE

Saturday Lotto

$15,569.55

⑈3456986⑈ 082⑆001⑆5699⑆0914⑈ 9

Heck, even $10,658.70 helps …

CONGRATULATIONS!

Postal Address: PO Box 6687, Silverwater NSW 2128 Web address: www.nswlotteries.com.au Telephone: 1300 363 444 Facsimile: (612) 02 9752 5516

041

TERRY FISHER
PO Box 196
BOND UNIVERSITY QLD 4229

POWERBALL

CHEQUE DATE 26/12/2007 CHEQUE NO. 6002315 PRN:

DRAW DATE	TSN	AMOUNT
14 Dec 2007	3998-04037123-127725	$10,658.70

Total: $10,658.70

All registered prizes up to $1,000, now including Lucky Lotteries can be collected from your local NSW Lotteries agency for up to EIGHT weeks after the draw.

Cash prizes up to $1,000 may be collected from any NSW Lotteries Agent up to 8 weeks after the draw.

RESULTS AND DIVIDENDS **POWERBALL HOTLINE: 1900 956 886**

(44c per minute Legion Interactive), 24 hours. Higher rates apply for mobile and public phones.

Lotto POWERBALL OZ LOTTO Strike instant scratchies Lucky Lotteries

Is Gambling a problem for you? Call G-line (NSW) counselling service 1800 633 635

NSW Lotteries

NSW LOTTERIES CORPORATION ABN 27 410 374 474

Westpac

WESTPAC BANKING CORPORATION
NSW GOVERNMENT DEPT. LEVEL 3, 275 KENT ST SYDNEY NSW

26/12/2007
6002315

Pay TERRY FISHER Or Order

The Sum of Ten thousand six hundred and fifty eight Dollars and 70 Cents

NOT NEGOTIABLE

For and on behalf of
Powerball Prize Fund Account

POWERBALL

$10,658.70

MA Howell

⑈6002315⑈ 032⑆001⑆ 115754⑈ 9

I'm sure you get the idea, so we'll stop showing off now.

Over several years we have tried a lot of different approaches to winning the lottery. While most of the ideas were mine, feedback and input from the Lotto Club members I worked with was always encouraged.

Later on I partnered with an Accredited Lotto Agent, who added his ideas to the melting pot.

Over the years, we have tossed away many ideas that did not work, and kept researching – and playing - the ones that showed most promise.

Invariably, the more successful approaches were when we **ORGANIZED all of the numbers**, rather than trying to PICK the winning numbers.

So – How Can We Help You Win MegaMillions?

MEGA MILLION ODDS EXPLAINED

The Odds of You Winning MegaMillions are:

1-in-175,711,536 for a single game.

However, the Odds of Winning the **Five Main Numbers** in MegaMillions are 1-in-3,819,816.

Here is our first secret to **Improving the Odds of Winning MegaMillions**. You see, every single one of those 3,819,816 Five-Number combinations can be played with all 46 Mega Balls.

Multiply 3,819,816 by 46 - and you get the overall odds of 175,711,536 for winning McgaMillions.

The sensible approach is to take it one-ball-at-a-time.

You can guarantee getting all five main balls by playing the numbers 1 to 56 in just 12 games – This is the kind of approach that has netted me two Million-Dollar-Plus Lotto wins and 5 main numbers & 4 numbers plus the Powerball in Australia's Powerball game – And the basis of our **Winning MegaMillions System**.

Taking it up a step, you can play 46 games and Guarantee getting the Mega Ball *IF* you play all 46 Mega Balls. This would Guarantee at least 20 Winning Numbers from the 5 main balls, IF you played all 56 balls at least 4 times.

However, because we create our own Winning MegaMillions Systems, we would push it a little further and get a **Triple Guarantee from a 50-game Mega Millions entry.**

The first Guarantee is the one we just mentioned – 20 Winning Numbers from the 5 main balls, spread over our 50 games.

Then we maximize our 50 games to make sure we have **at least two winning MegaMillions numbers together** (this is possible with 50 games, but not with 46).

Finally, we play all 46 Mega balls to Guarantee getting the Mega ball

While the larger of these Winning MegaMillions Systems (50 games) only guarantees a small win, it is a start to winning a bigger Mega Millions prize.

Getting 2 winning numbers is 40% of the way to getting 5 winning numbers – And we can GUARANTEE 2 or more winning numbers in just 50 Games. Plus the Mega Ball – which means a win of some kind.

The next thing people ask me for is a MegaMillions System to Guarantee 3 or more Winning MegaMillions Numbers.

Let me explain why this is not a value-for-money solution – I can do it, but I do not recommend it. Here is why.

> ***To give a 100% Guarantee of 3 or more winning MegaMillions numbers requires 1,380 Games. For a Guaranteed 3-number MegaMillions payout, NOT a good idea.***

WORKING WITHIN YOUR MEGAMILLIONS BUDGET

We strongly stress playing within your means.

There are Two Options for Sensible Play – And this book gives you Templates for both.

First, 23 Mega Millions games, that guarantee you have at least TEN Winning MegaMillions Numbers from the main 5 MegaMillions numbers.

We suggest for the Mega ball itself, you play all 23 Odd or all 23 Even Mega Balls; this gives you a 50/50 chance of getting the Mega Ball also. For the main 5 MegaMillions numbers, your 23 games give you a better than 80% chance of getting at least 2 numbers together, using our proprietary copyright system.

Second, 50 Mega Millions games, that guarantee you have at least TWENTY Winning MegaMillions Numbers from the main 5 MegaMillions numbers, plus a Guarantee that a minimum of at least 2 main MegaMillions numbers will be together.

By playing all 46 Mega Balls, you can also Guarantee getting the Mega ball.

Later in the book we also give you some general advice on setting up a Lotto Club (Lotto Syndicate) based on our experiences of running Group Entries.

So, let's move on to your 23-game System ....

23 MegaMillions games that guarantee you have at least TEN Winning MegaMillions Numbers from the main 5 MegaMillions numbers

Basic Numbers – Please See "Transpose" on Next Page.

1	2	32	41	53
1	12	13	51	52
1	26	27	35	45
2	24	28	45	52
3	10	13	17	53
3	25	38	44	49
4	17	36	48	49
4	18	33	50	54
5	8	31	38	48
5	19	39	40	55
6	18	34	37	56
6	19	24	32	47
7	11	27	29	43
7	20	21	46	55
8	14	25	37	47
9	12	21	42	43
9	16	30	34	46
10	26	28	41	51
11	20	23	30	42
14	29	31	35	44
15	22	36	39	54
15	32	40	50	56
16	22	23	33	56

Do **NOT** use these numbers as they are – Please see next page.

MAKING YOUR NUMBERS UNIQUE – TRANSPOSING YOUR NUMBERS

If you do use the numbers on Page 14 just as they are – You will probably have the same numbers as dozens, maybe hundreds, who did not change a few of their numbers to make their numbers unique. The fewer winners there are, the more you win - MAKE YOUR NUMBERS YOURS!

All 56 numbers appear at least twice – With 1, 32 and 56 appearing 3 times. This ensures your 23 games will generate at least 10 winning numbers from the main 5 MegaMillions Numbers – No matter what numbers are drawn.

To make your numbers YOURS, you need to TRANSPOSE (Swap) some of the numbers on Page 14. Use the Table below to do so; instructions are over the page.

Original Number:					
Change With:					
Original Number:					
Change With:					
Original Number:					
Change With:					

Here is an example:

Original Number:	5	13	20	35	42
Change With:	7	19	27	36	55

So first we find all lines with 5 –

~~5~~ 7	8	31	38	48
~~5~~ 7	19	39	40	55

And change the 5 to a 7

Then we need to find all lines that originally had 7 and change it to 5, as follows:

~~7~~ 5	11	27	29	43
~~7~~ 5	20	21	46	55

Just by swapping 5 and 7, four of the 23 games are now different.

We recommend swapping between 10 and 20 numbers, using the boxes on Page 15, to create numbers that are uniquely yours.

Occasionally you may try to change two numbers that are in the same game – either ignore it or use a different number.

The IMPORTANT part is to change enough numbers so that your games look different to the original set. You <u>MUST</u> swap both numbers (5 and 7 in our example above) to make sure all 56 numbers appear at least twice.

First, photocopy both pages 14 and 15. Then add 10 numbers to the Transpose Table. Now use a pen/pencil to change numbers in the 23 games, ticking them off as you go. Here is a Worked Example.

Original Number:	~~5~~	~~13~~	~~20~~	~~35~~	~~42~~
Change With:	~~7~~	~~19~~	~~27~~	~~36~~	~~55~~

1	2	32	41	53
1	12	13 (19)	51	52
1	26	27 (20)	35 (36)	45
2	24	28	45	52
3	10	13 (19)	17	53
3	25	38	44	49
4	17	36 (35)	48	49
4	18	33	50	54
5 (7)	8	31	38	48
5 (7)	19 (13)	39	40	55 (42)
6	18	34	37	56
6	19 (13)	24	32	47
7 (5)	11	27 (20)	29	43
7 (5)	20 (27)	21	46	55 (42)
8	14	25	37	47
9	12	21	42 (55)	43
9	16	30	34	46
10	26	28	41	51
11	20 (27)	23	30	42 (55)
14	29	31	35 (36)	44
15	22	36 (35)	39	54
15	32	40	50	56
16	22	23	33	56

As you can see on Page 17, swapping 10 numbers changed 13 of the 23 games (depending on the numbers you choose it could be more or less than 13 games – 2 of the changes resulted in 3 numbers being changed in the same game).

Because we will be randomly adding Mega Balls (see next page), this will also make your final 5+1 game different to other peoples.

Are the changes enough? For me, no. I would continue swapping more numbers until every game had at least 1 changed number – but then, I am a bit of a perfectionist, still working on that ☺

Unless someone has the same 5 main numbers as you PLUS the same Mega Ball, it really does not make much difference to the Minor Prizes. BUT, if you have hit the Jackpot you will be a lot happier if there is only ONE Winner ☺

To change these 10 numbers took me around 5 minutes; changing 20 numbers should not take you more than 10 minutes and is a pretty simple job.

Can I do it for you? Yes, but it takes time and I have no more of that than you do, plus my life is pretty hectic even on a quiet day. If you insist, Please Paypal **$10** to **terryf@qldnet.com.au** and I will swap up to 30 numbers for you and email them back to in 3-5 days. This is a discount rate for readers of this book only, so please advise your book purchase details also when you order.

And so to the Mega Ball.

ADDING THE MEGA BALL TO YOUR 23 GAMES.

The use of 23 Games was part of our Strategic Approach.

There are 46 Mega Balls – 23 Odd and 23 Even.

Our recommendation is to have two sets of coupons, both with the same 23 games for the main 5 numbers, but one with 23 Odd Mega Balls and one with 23 Even Mega Balls.

You then play the set you think is most likely – Odds or Evens. Some weeks it will be a toss-of-a-coin, or gut instinct, thing; but some weeks after a long run of one, it is smart to play the other. Like tossing a coin, results even out eventually and runs tend not to be too long.

Alternatively, you can simply use your 23 favorite numbers with just one set of coupons.

Either way, apply the Mega Ball randomly – this helps to ensure your 5+1 entry is different to other people's entry.

Also, please see page 23 – which lists the Most Drawn Mega Balls over the last 500 Draws, just in case this is your preference.

50 MegaMillions games that guarantee you have at least TWENTY Winning MegaMillions Numbers from the main 5 MegaMillions numbers – AND that TWO OR MORE are Guaranteed together.

TWO OR MORE = 40% OF THE WAY
TO SECOND PRIZE!

1	3	24	41	49
1	6	7	42	49
1	8	31	39	54
1	17	21	35	42
2	5	6	25	34
2	7	20	34	50
2	15	22	29	56
2	32	34	44	48
3	8	31	41	42
3	17	21	41	54
3	25	35	39	41
4	8	17	38	43
4	10	12	18	36
4	12	23	28	36
4	13	27	36	52
4	18	28	36	51
4	30	36	45	46
4	33	36	40	47
5	7	32	33	44
5	11	20	32	44
5	38	48	50	53

Continued Over The Page …

6	7	20	25	48
6	25	32	44	50
8	21	24	31	35
8	35	42	49	54
9	11	15	29	55
9	11	19	22	38
9	14	19	29	37
9	16	29	38	53
9	26	29	43	56
10	13	28	30	40
10	23	51	53	56
10	27	28	46	47
10	28	33	45	52
11	14	16	37	56
11	26	37	43	53
12	13	45	47	51
12	27	30	33	51
12	40	46	51	52
13	18	23	33	46
14	15	26	37	38
14	22	43	53	55
15	16	19	43	53
16	22	26	37	55
17	21	31	39	49
17	24	39	42	54
18	23	27	40	45
18	23	30	47	52
19	26	38	55	56
20	24	34	48	50

TRANSPOSING YOUR NUMBERS (AGAIN)

Same Warning - If you do use the numbers on Pages 20-21 just as they are – You will probably have the same numbers as dozens, maybe hundreds, who did not change a few of their numbers to make their numbers unique. The fewer winners there are, the more money you win - MAKE YOUR NUMBERS YOURS!

The technique for swapping numbers is exactly the same as on Pages 15-18, so I am not going to bore you by repeating it again here.

One small difference – the Number Distribution:

4 Appears 7 times

36, 38 & 53 Appear 6 times

8, 9, 10, 11, 12, 17, 18, 23, 26, 28, 29, 33, 37, 52, 43, 51 & 56 all appear 5 times

All other numbers appear 4 times.

These slight changes were required to fulfill the Guarantee of TWO OR MORE WINNING NUMBERS TOGETHER.

Can I do it for you? Again, Yes. Please Paypal $15 to terryf@qldnet.com.au and I will swap up to 30 numbers for you and email them back to in 3-5 days. This is a discount rate for readers of this book only, so please advise your book purchase details also when you order.

ADDING THE MEGA BALL TO YOUR 50 GAMES.

With 46 Mega Balls you can mark each one once, and 4 of them a second time. Again, apply the Mega Ball randomly – this helps to ensure your 5+1 entry is different to other people's entry.

The history of the Mega Ball over the last 500 draws (at Nov 2011) shows the most drawn Mega Balls are:

9, 25 & 36 - All drawn 17 times

19 & 26 - Both drawn 15 times

2, 6, 7, 15, 21, 35, & 38 - All drawn 14 times

13, 18 & 29 - All drawn 13 times

41 & 42 - Both drawn 12 times

10, 12, 20, 22, 24, 40, 44, 45 - All drawn 11 times

So – If you are playing the 23-Game version on page 14, you now know the most drawn 23 Mega balls if you prefer to use them.

Running Your Own Lotto Club

(Also known as a Lotto Syndicate in some places)

Practical Aspects, Winnings, Unpaid Shares & Costs Involved

The two big ways to improve your chances of winning are playing systematically and playing in a Lottery Club (Syndicate in some countries). For me, the two go together, in most cases. The cost of the larger Systems means you **have** to play in a Lottery Club. A Lottery Club can be anything from two people upwards. I personally prefer between six and ten members, with 20-30 for a large Jackpot or SuperDraw.

Trouble is, most Lottery Clubs fall apart fairly quickly. This chapter highlights why and what you need to do to run one properly.

Essentials:

Written Record of Members, their payments into the Lottery Club, and the payment of Winnings to them.

Written Rules, preferably signed by Lottery Club Members.

Preferred:

A Bank Account specifically for the Lottery Club.

Photocopies of Coupons for all Members

Written Record of Members

Absolutely essential. By recording payments you know who has paid, who hasn't, and what winnings have been paid to whom.

One of the most contentious issues is unpaid Shares. I personally believe your Rules should state, quite clearly, that if you are not fully paid up – you are not in the Lottery Club for that week. Great friendships suffer on the altar of money. If someone misses for 4 weeks and your Lottery Club wins – they expect their Share (take what I owe out of my winnings!) If someone misses for 4 weeks and your Lottery Club does **not** win – the arrears get too big to pay and they drop out. Guess who usually ends up making good the shortage? The organizer, not surprisingly, tires of this after getting caught a couple of times – and the Lottery Club folds.

Have written Rules, signed by Members, acknowledging they accept that if they are not fully paid up, they are not in it for that week!

So what do you do with unpaid Shares? The Rules should spell it out quite clearly. My preference is pooling. Members collectively share the cost and share the winnings. You will see I suggest having a Bank Account. Members should pay slightly more than they need, establishing a Reserve Fund. If there is a Share unpaid, it should be paid from this Reserve Fund (rather than the Lottery Club Organiser dipping into his own pocket) and Members should then share any winnings equally.

If the Organizer – or any other Member - agrees to pick up unpaid Shares, they are entitled to the Winnings. If you prefer this, the Rules should say so.

The other reason for the Bank Account is the costs involved. Usually one person gets all the work. And all the costs. Not good enough. If some-one does all the work, they are entitled to be reimbursed for any costs involved. This may include any or all of the following:

> Photocopies for members, stationery, postage,
> phone calls, faxes, etc.

For a large Lottery Club (say 20 people) the Members may agree that the one doing all the work gets a Free Share in return for their time. This is particularly useful if you also agree each Member will take a share in running the Lottery Club – say one month each. This gives all Members a chance for a free month in return for their time – and brings home to everyone the time and hassle involved!

What about paying out winnings? I believe anything below $20 per Member should go into the Bank Account for Jackpots and SuperDraws. Whether you are playing for a $100 Million Jackpot or $1 Million, the odds are the same - and so is the cost of playing. Technically, the smartest way to play Lotto is to save up every week and play only SuperDraws and large Jackpots - but of course most of us Lotto enthusiasts need the "weekly fix!" Marrying these two needs, why not put all weekly winnings under $20 per Member into a special SuperDraw Bank Account? Winnings over $20 per Member per week are paid out. With larger wins paid out immediately and smaller wins accumulated for big draws, you get the best of both worlds.

You will also need to decide whether you keep the same numbers or change them occasionally.

Finally, to prove he/she actually put the coupons on, the Organizer should provide photocopies to all Members. If you are a small Lottery Club – especially family or working in the same place – simply showing them the coupons is obviously fine.

A set of Specimen Rules is provided overleaf. **These are provided for guidance only and are not intended to constitute legal advice - please seek proper legal advice.**

SPECIMEN ONLY - GOVERNING RULES.

NAME OF LOTTERY CLUB:

SYSTEM PLAYED & WEEKLY COST:

MEMBER'S NAME:

ADDRESS:

PHONE:

1. The Lottery Club shall be limited to Ten (10) Members only.
2. There shall be ten (10) equal shares of $10.00 per week.
3. Membership shall be for a minimum of five weeks, with cancellation of Membership subject to two (2) weeks Notice.
4. A Bank Account entitled "xx Lottery Club" shall be established and operated by (Name/s). To ensure a complete audit trail all financial transactions will pass through this Account.
5. I agree to pay weekly (or monthly) in full, (1 day in advance for cash, 7 days in advance for cheques). **I agree that where Members subscriptions are not received before the Draw, Members are not financial for that week.**
6. All Winnings under $20 per week per Member shall be paid into the Bank Account. All Winnings over $20 per week per Member shall be paid out. The balance of the Bank Account one week before a SuperDraw (Jackpot) shall be used for a special SuperDraw entry.
7. I accept that the Organizer gets a free Share in return for their time. Organizing the Lottery Club will be done on a rotational monthly basis.

8. All costs incurred, including photocopies for members, stationery, postage, computer consumables, phone calls and faxes etc will be met by applying $1 per member, from each weekly subscription, towards expenses.
9. The numbers will be reviewed monthly and may be changed / Numbers will not be changed once established
10. This Agreement is intended by all Members signing it to be legally binding.
11. Amendment of these Rules shall be Subject to the Agreement of a Minimum of two-thirds of all Lottery Club Members

In signing this form, I confirm I have read the Rules for this Lottery Club and accept them.

Signed: ______________ ______ Date: _________

This, of course, is only a specimen set of rules to give you some ideas and is not intended to constitute legal advice. Please feel free to adapt it to whatever your members agree on. If in any doubt, seek proper legal advice.

Good Luck with your Mega Millions entries.

A copy of all of our websites appears on Page 2; if you need a system for another lottery it is almost certainly on one of those sites.

I can be contacted by email at ***terryf@qldnet.com.au***
This is also my PayPal email if you want me to personalize your numbers for you, $10 for the 23 games and $15 for the 50 games.

Good Luck & Best Wishes,

Terry Fisher, Double Million-Dollar Lottery Winner

Other Great Lottery Products Available On The Web Include –

Discover the Systems and Strategies the Experts Use - Explode your chances of Winning the Big One with....

"Winning Lotto - Secrets" - Pro Version

www.lottery-and-lotto.com

Instant Download

Stunning New Book Reveals The Worlds
Most Powerful And Secret Formula
For Improving Your Odds of Winning Lotto

<u>The Ultimate Lottery Guide</u> –

"The Only Way To Win At Lotto"

from Robert Serotic.

The most comprehensive Lotto Book ever written.

288 pages, 222 different Lotto Systems.

Cover Price, $39.95 – FREE Postage Worldwide

<u>PRINTED</u> Version only – sent Airmail.

http://www.lottomasta.com/serotic-lottery-book.html

A Disappearing Classic – Only a few copies remain worldwide, and I have most of them.

Maximise Your Chances in the next Powerball Jackpot!

"Powerball Strategies – Pro Version."

The specialist "PICK-5" Book, suitable for any Pick-5 or Pick-5 + 1 Lottery worldwide, including Powerball, Mega Millions, California Lotto, etc.

Offers 19 different Pick-5 Systems.

http://www.Powerballpro.com

Instant Download

PROSPERITY CONSCIOUSNESS IS EVERYTHING!

A Free Gift, Highly Recommended :

THE SCIENCE OF GETTING RICH - 100% Free

(You do have to sign up, but I make no money on this. It is simply a book I downloaded for free and fully endorse).

http://www.scienceofgettingrich.net/subscribe.html

THIS IS "THE SECRET" BEHIND THE "THE SECRET" – If you have seen The Secret DVD or read the book – THIS is the book they are talking about at the beginning – YOURS FREE!

"The ownership of money and property comes as a result of doing things in a certain way. Those who do things in this certain way, whether on purpose or accidentally, get rich. Those who do not do things in this certain way, no matter how hard they work or how able they are, remain poor."

Wallace D Wattles

The Surest Way To Remain Poor Is To Think Poor!

www.ingramcontent.com/pod-product-compliance
Lightning Source LLC
LaVergne TN
LVHW010549100826
845148LV00013B/2667

* 9 7 8 1 4 7 0 9 6 6 5 1 5 *